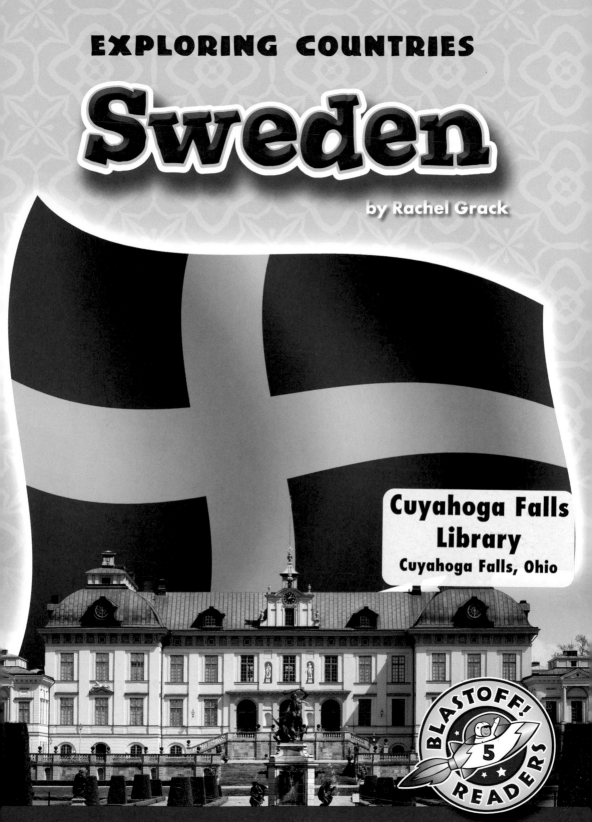

EXPLORING COUNTRIES

Sweden

by Rachel Grack

BLASTOFF!
5
READERS

BELLWETHER MEDIA · MINNEAPOLIS, MN

Note to Librarians, Teachers, and Parents:

Blastoff! Readers are carefully developed by literacy experts and combine standards-based content with developmentally appropriate text.

Level 1 provides the most support through repetition of high-frequency words, light text, predictable sentence patterns, and strong visual support.

Level 2 offers early readers a bit more challenge through varied simple sentences, increased text load, and less repetition of high-frequency words.

Level 3 advances early-fluent readers toward fluency through increased text and concept load, less reliance on visuals, longer sentences, and more literary language.

Level 4 builds reading stamina by providing more text per page, increased use of punctuation, greater variation in sentence patterns, and increasingly challenging vocabulary.

Level 5 encourages children to move from "learning to read" to "reading to learn" by providing even more text, varied writing styles, and less familiar topics.

Whichever book is right for your reader, Blastoff! Readers are the perfect books to build confidence and encourage a love of reading that will last a lifetime!

This edition first published in 2011 by Bellwether Media, Inc.

No part of this publication may be reproduced in whole or in part without written permission of the publisher. For information regarding permission, write to Bellwether Media, Inc., Attention: Permissions Department, 5357 Penn Avenue South, Minneapolis, MN 55419.

Library of Congress Cataloging-in-Publication Data

Koestler-Grack, Rachel A., 1973-
  Sweden / by Rachel Grack.
    p. cm. – (Blastoff! readers: Exploring countries)
  Includes bibliographical references and index.
  Summary: "Developed by literacy experts for students in grades three through seven, this book introduces young readers to the geography and culture of Sweden"–Provided by publisher.
  ISBN 978-1-60014-490-5 (hardcover : alk. paper)
  1. Sweden–Juvenile literature. 2. Sweden–Social life and customs–Juvenile literature. I. Title.
  DL609.K595 2010
  948.5–dc22   2010009217

Printed in the United States of America, North Mankato, MN.

080110   1162

Contents

073

Sweden is part of the Scandinavian **Peninsula** in northern Europe. It is the fourth-largest country in Europe, covering 173,859 square miles (450,295 square kilometers). Sweden shares the Scandinavian Peninsula with Norway, its neighbor to the west, and the northwestern part of Finland, its neighbor to the east. The capital of Sweden is Stockholm.

! **fun fact**

Some of Sweden is so far north that the sun never completely sets during the summer! Swedes call that region the "Land of the Midnight Sun."

Sweden has 2,000 miles (3,218 kilometers) of coastline. The Baltic Sea and the **Gulf** of Bothnia lie to the east of Sweden. The Danish Straits separate Sweden from Denmark, a country to the southwest. The North Sea lies off of Sweden's southwest coast.

Sweden's land features range from flat plains to towering mountains. Rugged, snow-capped mountains and **glaciers** cover the land in the far north. The Fjällen Mountains run along the border between Norway and Sweden. Traveling through these mountains is dangerous because of frequent **avalanches**. Southern Sweden is made up of plains and forests. Most Swedes live in southern Sweden, where the plains and river valleys create rich farmland.

The coastline offers both sandy beaches and rocky shores. Scandinavian countries are famous for their many **fjords**. In Sweden, these inlets of water can be found all along the Baltic Sea coast.

! fun fact
Sweden has over 90,000 lakes!

Fjällen Mountains

In May 2009, Polar World opened in Dalarna, Sweden. Covering more than 440,000 square feet (41,000 square meters), it is the world's largest polar bear park. It includes a large deep-water area and a place for bears to hunt for fish. Polar World even has machines to make snow!

Polar World is the first polar bear park focused on breeding the bears. In the wild, there are about 20,000 to 25,000 polar bears. They are not in danger of **extinction** right now. However, some scientists think the number of polar bears in the wild is beginning to fall. Polar World is a chance to make sure these animals continue to thrive.

Did you know?

Polar bears have clear, hollow hair follicles. Their fur traps the sun's heat and keeps them warm in cold weather.

moose

Many animals live in Sweden. Reindeer, roe deer, and moose can be found throughout the country. Sweden has one of the largest moose populations on Earth. Moose are so common there that they can be a driving hazard.

wolf

wolverine

Did you know?

Sweden has only a few hundred wolves and wolverines left in the wild. The country has passed laws to protect these and other endangered animals.

kingfisher

Birds fly above the many landscapes of Sweden. Owls, grouse, hawks, woodpeckers, and buzzards live around mountains and forests. Kingfishers make their nests near rivers and streams. Colorful ducks and water birds gather on Sweden's lakes and seacoasts.

The People

Over 9 million people live in Sweden today. Many of them came to Sweden from other European countries. People from Finland, called Finns, make up the largest group of **immigrants**. Other large groups of immigrants have come from Denmark and Germany. Recently, people have come to Sweden from countries in the Middle East and Asia. Swedish is the official language of Sweden. Finnish is also a common language in certain parts of the country.

Speak Swedish!

English	Swedish	How to say it
hello	hej	HAY
good-bye	hej då	HAY-doh
yes	ja	YAH
no	nej	NAY
please	snälla	snell-ah
thank you	tack	TAHK
friend	vän	ven

Did you know?
In 1906, Sweden reformed its spelling system to make words easier to spell. For example, the letter *K* replaced the letter *Q*. The letter *Z* is rarely used.

The Sami are **native** to Sweden. They were once **nomads**, following reindeer herds from place to place. Today, the Sami live a more settled lifestyle. Many of them still speak their native language. In the summertime, some practice their traditional nomadic lifestyle. They follow reindeer herds from the forests to the mountains.

fun fact

Some Swedes who live in the city also own places in the countryside where they can go to relax.

Most Swedes live in the central and southern parts of the country, where the land is good for farming and the climate is mild. Many people live in and around Stockholm. In cities, most people live in tall apartment buildings. They get around town on foot or ride metro trains, motorcycles, or bicycles. They shop at markets, small stores, and malls. Swedes who live in the countryside often live in farmhouses. They travel to small villages or cities to do their shopping.

Where People Live in Sweden

countryside 15%

cities 85%

Sweden has an excellent railway system. This makes travel easy, even for Swedes who live in rural areas. The trains are **energy efficient**. A network of roads and highways also allows Swedes to drive around the country with ease.

Most children in Sweden begin school at age 6. Students start *grundskola*, or elementary school, at age 7. They attend *grundskola* until they are 16. Children study reading, math, science, and social studies. They also take classes in music, art, and physical education.

High school, or *gymnasieskola*, begins after *grundskola*. Students choose whether or not they want to go to high school. All high school programs take three years to complete. Students who do not go to high school often attend a two-year school that prepares them for a specific area of work. About three out of ten high school graduates choose to go to university.

fun fact
All schooling is free in Sweden, including university.

Did you know?
Uppsala University is the oldest university in Sweden. It was founded in 1477.

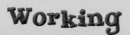

Where People Work in Sweden

manufacturing 28.2%

farming 1.1%

services 70.7%

Sweden's **natural resources** offer several opportunities for work. Many Swedes are miners or loggers. Sweden is one of the world's top producers of iron ore. Sweden also makes wood products, including paper, wood pulp, and lumber. Farmers grow wheat, sugar beets, and potatoes. They also raise cattle, hogs, and **poultry**. Some Swedes find work as fishermen along Sweden's long coastline.

Cities also offer plenty of work for Swedes. Factories manufacture machinery, tools, chemicals, and automobiles. Most Swedes have **service jobs**. They work in hotels, restaurants, and stores.

fun fact

The Swedish government passed a law that allows people to walk, bike, or camp anywhere in Sweden's countryside.

Swedes enjoy spending time outdoors. Downhill and cross-country skiing are favorite sports in Sweden. Families often spend weekends camping and exploring the land.

Many people hike the *Kungsleden*, or King's Trail. This 270-mile (440-kilometer) hiking trail runs through northern Sweden.

Orienteering is one of Sweden's most popular sports. In this sport, cross-country runners try to find their way through a variety of unfamiliar landscapes. They use only a map and a compass to guide them. Swedish children also enjoy the game of bandy. Played on ice, the game is similar to hockey. However, a ball is used instead of a puck.

bandy

Swedes consume the largest amount of coffee per person in the world. The average Swede uses about 17.5 pounds (8 kilograms) of coffee beans each year.

fun fact

The word *smörgåsbord* means "a table full of sandwiches."

Swedish meals often feature meat or fish with potatoes. Swedish meatballs are a mixture of beef, pork, breadcrumbs, and onions. They are often soaked in milk or cream and served with gravy. *Pyttipanna* is a dish made with potatoes, onions, and leftover meats. Herring, a fish caught off the coasts of Sweden, is also used in many dishes. It is often **pickled** and eaten alone or with crackers. Herring is also a popular item in a *smörgåsbord*, a buffet that includes a variety of Swedish foods.

Swedes have a coffee break, or *fika*, a few times a day. They drink strong coffee or tea and talk with friends or coworkers. *Kaffebröd*, or coffee bread, is usually eaten during a *fika*. These pastries are sweet and have almond, cinnamon, or fruit flavorings.

swedish meatballs

pickled herring

Did you know?
Girls who want to become the national Lucia must enter a competition that judges their singing of carols and gospels.

Many religious holidays are celebrated in Sweden. The month-long Christmas celebration starts with Saint Lucia Day on December 13. Each home chooses a girl to be the Lucia, or "Queen of Light." She wears a long, white dress and a crown of electric candles on her head. There is also a Lucia for each town and one for the nation. The Christmas feast includes a *smörgåsbord* of traditional foods. Christmas toffee called *knäck* is a holiday treat.

Sweden also has many national holidays. The National Day of Sweden is on June 6. It celebrates the founding of the country. Midsummer's Eve is another holiday celebrated all over Sweden. This festival takes place on the **summer solstice**. Swedes dance around a **maypole** in hopes of a large harvest in the fall. The event also includes traditional Swedish music, food, and clothing.

maypole →

fun fact

The oldest glassworks factory in Sweden is Kosta Boda. It was founded in 1742.

Sweden is famous for its crafts and inventions. Swedish crystal and glassware are sold around the world. Glassblowers create colorful and artistic glass pieces by hand. In the winter, glassworks factories invite travelers and locals inside to warm up. This tradition is called *hyttsill*.

Swedes have provided the world with many new inventions. These include the **safety match** and the propeller. The most famous Swedish inventor is Alfred Nobel, who invented **dynamite** and also started the Nobel Prize tradition. Each year, select people are awarded a special prize for their achievements in science, medicine, literature, and peace. These awards are reminders of Sweden's history, culture, and contributions to the world.

Alfred Nobel

Nobel awards ceremony

Fast Facts About Sweden

Sweden's Flag

The Swedish flag is blue with a yellow cross. The colors come from the Swedish coat of arms, which was blue and had three yellow crowns on it. The design for the flag has been around for hundreds of years, but the flag was officially adopted in 1906.

Official Name: Kingdom of Sweden

Area: 173,859 square miles
(450,295 square kilometers);
Sweden is the 55th largest
country in the world.

Capital City:	Stockholm
Important Cities:	Göteborg, Malmö, Uppsala, Linköping
Population:	9,074,055 (July 2010)
Official Language:	Swedish
National Holiday:	National Day of Sweden (June 6)
Religions:	Lutheran (87%), Other (13%)
Major Industries:	manufacturing, mining, forestry, services, tourism
Natural Resources:	iron ore, copper, lead, wood, zinc
Manufactured Products:	iron and steel, wood products, machinery, food products, glassware, cutlery, clothing, cars
Farm Products:	barley, wheat, sugar beets, potatoes, milk, poultry, pork
Unit of Money:	krona; the krona is divided into 100 öre.

Glossary

avalanches—large masses of snow or ice that suddenly break away from and slide down the sides of mountains

dynamite—an explosive

energy efficient—uses little energy to function

extinction—when every member of a species has died off

fjords—long, narrow inlets of water between steep cliffs; fjords are formed by the movement of glaciers.

glaciers—massive sheets of ice that cover a large area of land

gulf—a part of an ocean or sea that extends into land

immigrants—people who leave one country to live in another country

maypole—a tall pole that is often decorated and used in celebrations of Midsummer's Eve

native—originally from a place

natural resources—materials in the earth that are taken out and used to make products or fuel

nomads—people who have no specific home and travel from place to place

peninsula—a section of land that extends out from a larger piece of land and is almost completely surrounded by water

pickled—preserved with pickle; pickle is a liquid that keeps food from spoiling.

poultry—birds raised for their eggs or meat

safety match—a match that will only light on a special surface

service jobs—jobs that perform tasks for people or businesses

summer solstice—the date when summer begins

To Learn More

AT THE LIBRARY

Fast, April, and Keltie Thomas. *Sweden: the Culture*. New York, N.Y.: Crabtree Publishing, 2004.

Grahame, Deborah A. *Sweden*. New York, N.Y.: Marshall Cavendish Benchmark, 2007.

Yanuck, Debbie L. *Sweden*. Mankato, Minn.: Blue Earth Books, 2004.

ON THE WEB

Learning more about Sweden is as easy as 1, 2, 3.

1. Go to www.factsurfer.com.

2. Enter "Sweden" into the search box.

3. Click the "Surf" button and you will see a list of related Web sites.

With factsurfer.com, finding more information is just a click away.

Index

The images in this book are reproduced through the courtesy of: Mikael Damkier, front cover; Maisei Raman, front cover (flag), p. 28; Johan Epparson, pp. 4-5; Chad Ehlers/Photolibrary, pp. 6-7, 16-17, 24, 26, 27; vario images GmbH & Co.KG/Alamy, p. 7 (small); Veronika Vasilyuk, p. 8; Helen E. Grose, p. 9; Michael Breuer/Photolibrary, pp. 10-11; Juan Martinez, pp. 11 (top), 15, 18, 21, 23 (top & bottom); Wendy Nero, p. 11 (middle); Karel Gallas, p. 11 (bottom); Arctic Images/Alamy, p. 13; Aleksi Markku, p. 14; Andrei Nekrassov, p. 15 (small); Bjorn Svensson/Photolibrary, p. 19 (left); Andre Maslennikov/Photolibrary, p. 19 (right); Norbert Eisele-Hein/Photolibrary, p. 20; Alena Ozerova, p. 22; WoodyStock/Alamy, p. 25; Keystone Archives/Photolibrary, p. 27 (small); Freddy Eliasson, p. 29 (bill & coin).